OLD WORLD MONKEYS

Ann Baggaley

Grolier
an imprint of
◼SCHOLASTIC
www.scholastic.com/librarypublishing

Published 2009 by Grolier
An imprint of Scholastic Library Publishing
Old Sherman Turnpike, Danbury,
Connecticut 06816

For The Brown Reference Group plc
Project Editor: Jolyon Goddard
Picture Researcher: Clare Newman
Designers: Dave Allen, Jeni Child, Lynne Ross,
John Dinsdale, Sarah Williams
Managing Editors: Bridget Giles, Tim Harris

Volume ISBN-13: 978-0-7172-8029-2
Volume ISBN-10: 0-7172-8029-2

**Library of Congress
Cataloging-in-Publication Data**

Nature's children. Set 4.
    p. cm.
  Includes bibliographical references and
index.
  ISBN 13: 978-0-7172-8083-4
  ISBN 10: 0-7172-8083-7 ((set 4) : alk. paper)
  I. Animals--Encyclopedias, Juvenile. I.
  Grolier (Firm)
  QL49.N385 2009
  590.3--dc22
                        2007046315

Printed and bound in China

PICTURE CREDITS

Front Cover: **Shutterstock**: Michael Lynch.

Back Cover: **Nature PL**: Bernard Castelein,
Matthew Maran, Anup Shah.

Nature PL: Bernard Castelein 18,
Christophe Courteau 17, Matthew Maran
42, Anup Shah 9, 10, 29, 41, Mike Wilkes 13,
Rod Williams 6, Jean-Pierre Zwaenepoel 14;
Photolibrary.com: Kerstin Layer 45;
Shutterstock: Henk Bentlage 37, Franck
Camhi 5, EML 2–3, Peter Masek 34, Dmitrijs
Mihejevs 4, Kirby Morgan 46, Steffen Foerster
Photography 22, 26–27, 30, Johan Swanepoel
33, Ronald Van Der Beek 21, Yury
Zaporozhchenko 38.

Contents

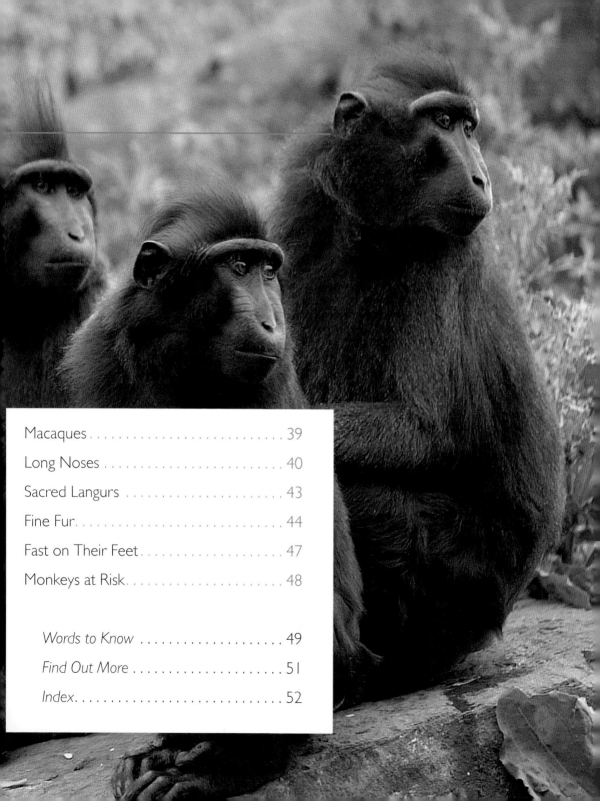

FACT FILE: Old World Monkeys

Class	Mammals (Mammalia)
Order	Lemurs, tarsiers, monkeys, and apes (Primates)
Family	Old World monkeys (Cercopithecidae)
Genera	18 genera
Species	116 species
World distribution	Africa and Asia
Habitat	Forests, grasslands, mountains, and scrublands
Distinctive physical characteristics	Downward opening nostrils; limbs of equal length; opposable thumbs; some species have a bare backside
Habits	Active during the day; live in social groups; most species live in trees, a few species live on the ground
Diet	Leaves, fruit, seeds, bark, flowers, roots, and bulbs; in some species, insects and small mammals; occasionally fish and shellfish

Introduction

Across Africa and Asia—the Old World—there is an amazing variety of monkeys. They live in rain forests, on grasslands, and in the foothills of the highest mountains. Almost always, they are seen in noisy gatherings of family and friends. Old World monkeys come in many shapes, sizes, and colors. Some are large and powerful, a tough match for any lion or tiger. Others are shy, slender acrobats of the treetops. Monkeys of several different types often peacefully share a **territory**, as long as they are not in competition for the same food.

Vervet monkeys are found in Africa, where they live in small groups.

The Douc langur is a rare monkey that lives in Vietnam, Laos, and Cambodia.

Old and New

There are two main groups of monkeys: Old World monkeys, which live in Africa and Asia; and New World Monkeys, which come from Central and South America.

There are important differences between these groups. New World monkeys have a flat nose with nostrils opening to the sides. Old World monkeys have a narrow nose with nostrils that point downward, like humans. Another difference is their tails. Many New World monkeys have a long **prehensile** (PREE-HEN-SUHL) tail—a flexible tail that serves as an extra limb for holding onto branches or picking up things. Some Old World monkeys have a long tail and others have a short one, but none has a prehensile tail. However, nearly all of the Old World group have something just as useful—an **opposable thumb**. They can hold their thumb against their fingers to pick up objects, again like humans.

Many Old World monkeys also have a "seat pad" of tough bare skin on their backside. In some monkeys, the pad is brightly colored.

Varied Group

Monkeys are **primates**, which means they belong to the same order, or major group, as apes such as gorillas, chimpanzees, and humans. There are 116 **species**, or types, of Old World monkeys. They include monkeys that live mostly on the ground, such as macaques (MA-KAKS), baboons, and mandrills. Other old world monkeys live in trees, such as colobus monkeys, langurs, and leaf monkeys. These monkeys have been around for a long time. **Fossils** of monkeys dating back 15 million years have been found in Africa. Scientists have also discovered that a type of macaque lived in Europe more than two million years ago—though none is found there now.

Old World monkeys vary enormously in size, from large and solid to small and slim. Their coat of dense fur comes in dozens of different colors. Most Old World monkeys have arms and legs of almost equal length. That makes them agile and able to move fast.

The red colobus from
Zanzibar, islands off
the coast of eastern
Africa, has red, black,
and white fur.

Grivets are a type of vervet monkey. They live in Sudan, Ethiopia, and Eritrea.

Almost Everywhere

Old World monkeys are found in many countries. Various species are spread all over Africa, except for the very dry desert regions. India, Pakistan, and Bangladesh have many different kinds of monkeys, too. A variety of monkeys also appears in large numbers in southern China, Japan, and Southeast Asia, including Indonesia.

The majority of the Old World monkeys are tree-dwellers. They live in rain forests, woodlands, and scrublands. Most of them live in regions where the climate is warm all year round. Only a few hardy types of monkeys are able to survive cold, snowy winters. Those monkeys are found in highland areas, such as the foothills of the Himalayas and the mountains of northern Japan.

A few types of monkeys spend most of their time on the ground. Those include baboons, which roam the grasslands and bushlands of Africa. Other African ground-dwellers, the mandrills, prefer to live on forest floors.

Troops

It is rare for monkeys to live alone. Most of them live in a group, which is known as a **troop**. A troop may be anything from a family of just three or four, to a large community of more than a hundred monkeys. One of the most common arrangements is a troop consisting of one male and several females with their babies.

There is safety in numbers. One monkey always acts as a guard—keeping a lookout for danger. Sometimes, troops of different species of monkeys live together in close friendship. They even take turns on guard duty. While one troop visits an unsheltered place such as a water hole, the other species stays on guard for **predators**.

Of course, where there are a lot of monkeys, squabbles often break out over food, rank, or even friendships. However, serious fights are unusual. While many troops are welcoming toward one another, others are very protective of their personal territory. They chase away any other troop that comes too close.

There might be up to 150 monkeys in a troop of olive baboons.

Two Hanuman langurs from India hang out together.

14

Special Friends

Monkeys that live in large troops, such as baboons, often choose certain troop members as best friends. In the same way as humans, they like to spend time with someone special. Friendships between females are very common. Often male and female monkeys bond closely, too, even if they never **mate**.

Male and female friendships usually develop when a new male joins the troop. The male needs the troop to accept him, which might take many months. Faced with all these strangers, who may be hostile, he picks one female and tries to get her interest. Gradually, the female becomes used to having the male around and might eventually like him enough to be friends. Once the bond has been made, the male is likely to be seen as one of the family.

Monkey Meals

There seems to be no end to the list of things that monkeys like to eat. Different species have their particular preferences. Some are almost entirely plant-eating, or vegetarian, while others try anything they can get their hands on.

The forest-dwelling monkeys feed on the leaves, fruit, and seeds of trees and other plants. They also eat fungi, flowers, and tree bark, and dig up roots and bulbs. To add variety to their diet, some monkeys catch insects, birds, and small mammals. Macaques that live near rivers or the coast are known to eat fish, shellfish, and even seaweed. If there are cultivated fields nearby, monkeys have little hesitation in raiding a farmer's crops, and can do much damage.

Big, powerful baboons eat a lot of grass. But they also have an appetite for meat. They go hunting in groups for mammals such as hares and young gazelles.

When fresh grass is abundant, it makes up more than 90 percent of a Gelada baboon's diet.

A golden leaf monkey from India tries standing. When leaf monkeys come down from the trees, they usually scurry around on all fours.

Leaf Eaters

Colobus monkeys and leaf monkeys have special **adaptations** in their body to help with the huge amount of leaves that they eat.

Leaf eaters' teeth have a strong coating of enamel and their back teeth, or molars, have sharp points that cut through tough foliage. They also have a large stomach that is divided into special **sacs**. This big stomach can hold a lot of leaves. Because leaves are not very nutritious, the monkeys have to eat many of them to get all the energy they need to survive.

Leaf monkeys of various types are found all over Asia. Most of them are slender and agile, and many have a tail that is much longer than their body. Their names can be highly descriptive. Species such as the white-rumped black leaf monkey, golden leaf monkey, and dusky leaf monkey are colored in the way that their names suggest!

Making Faces

Like humans, monkeys have a very expressive face—they smile and yawn. However, the faces monkeys make do not always mean the same thing as they do in human faces. When a monkey gives a big grin it is not amused at anything. A grin is often a monkey's way of showing fear. Pulling back the lips to make an expression that looks like a smile can also be a sign of anger.

When a human makes a huge yawn it means he or she is bored or sleepy. To a monkey, yawning is a good way of displaying a mouthful of sharp teeth to an enemy or a rival. It says: "Keep away!"

A monkey also uses special expressions to attract a mate. It might push out its lips in a pout, click its tongue, or blow out its cheeks. A long steady stare sometimes does the trick, too.

A Barbary macaque bares its impressive teeth in an aggressive display.

A young Sykes' monkey from Africa calls to its mother.

Communication

As well as using facial expressions, monkeys communicate with one another by using their voices. Their calls can mean many things. For example, one sound might be a warning of danger and another might be used to challenge an intruder. Male monkeys that lead a troop often call loudly to get the other monkeys to behave. They also might call simply to say, "I'm here!" to other monkeys within earshot. Monkeys tend to be very noisy at dawn, when the troop wakes up, and again at dusk, when they settle to sleep. Their calls are a way of announcing that a territory is occupied.

Some monkeys shriek or bark with fear, rage, or excitement. A mother monkey usually responds quickly to the scream of a lost or frightened baby. Gentler sounds include chattering. A soft grunt might be used in friendship or by a monkey that wants to back down from a fight.

Grooming

Monkeys are busy, active animals. Feeding, searching for water, and watching for enemies takes up a lot of time. But they do allow some time for rest and relaxation.

When a troop takes a break, the monkeys often gather round for a peaceful **grooming** session. They comb carefully through one another's coat with their hands, picking out dirt and irritating pests. Often, they eat the insects as a snack! Mutual grooming, as it is called, usually occurs between monkeys that are close friends. As well as being a useful service, grooming helps strengthen bonds. It reduces the likelihood of stressful quarrels and keeps the monkeys united as a group or troop.

Female monkeys also spend a lot of time grooming their young. If a mother wants to groom a friend, she needs both hands free, so she passes her baby over to the friend to hold.

No Ceremony

Some monkeys, including baboons, can breed at any time of year. Others, such as the patas monkey, mate only throughout the rainy season. When there is plenty of rain, the plants on which many monkeys feed grow much faster. That means a good supply of food for all, and if food is abundant the monkeys are healthier, and, therefore, likely to breed successfully.

Monkeys do not usually have elaborate courtship ceremonies. Because they live in troops, they already know one another very well. Couples that pair up have often been friends for a long time. When monkeys court, most of them do little more than make a few faces or shake their head at one another.

In many species, the female makes the first approach. Female Hanuman langurs put some effort into getting a mate. If a male Hanuman langur does not appear to be interested, the female might hit or bite him to make him notice her!

26

A young baboon stays close to its mother for the first year of its life.

Newly Born

Female monkeys give birth to their young about five to seven months after mating. The **gestation period** depends on the species. The females do not make special nests for their young. A baby might be born in a tree or on the ground. There is usually only one monkey born at a time. On rare occasions, twins are born.

Newborn monkeys are fully covered with fur. At first, they might be a completely different color from their parents. For example, some dark-coated monkeys, such as langurs, give birth to a white or even a bright orange baby.

A mother monkey feeds her baby on her milk and carries it around everywhere for the first few weeks of its life. When the baby is very tiny, she holds it closely to her breast. Later, as the infant grows stronger, it might ride on its mother's back, clinging to her fur. Male monkeys sometimes carry a baby on their back, too.

A proboscis monkey from Borneo grooms her baby.

A pair of mother baboons rests while their young play with a piece of garbage. Baboons often raid human garbage bins for food.

In the Family

When a new baby is born into the troop, all the females take an interest. They want to touch it and help care for it. Although monkeys often babysit for one another, they are not always reliable "nannies." They often get bored, put the baby down, and wander off. Fortunately, the mother monkey is never far away and comes to the rescue.

One of the biggest dangers for baby monkeys comes from the adult males of their own species. If a powerful new male joins a troop, he will want to father his own young as soon as possible. He may ruthlessly kill babies in his new troop so that the females will be soon ready to breed again and have his babies.

Monkeys that survive infancy stop **nursing** from their mother when they are a year or two old. Then, they are nearly adults. That is often the time when the mother has a new baby. Mothers and daughters stay close to each other in the same troop for life. But when young male monkeys are fully grown they usually leave their family and find a new troop.

Enemies All Around

Although monkeys are smart and agile, they cannot always escape other animals that hunt them for **prey**. They have many dangerous enemies. Even monkeys that spend most of their life high in the treetops are never really safe.

Among the predators that forest-dwelling monkeys most fear are eagles. These huge birds swoop through the trees to snatch an unwary victim off its branch or the forest floor. Big eagles are strong enough to kill even the really big monkeys, such as mandrills.

Other enemies include pythons, leopards, and lions. Baboons, which live on the ground, are particularly common prey for the big cats, which kill baboons in large numbers.

When danger threatens, monkeys sound the alarm with loud calls. They are clever enough to use different sounds for different predators. For example, one call means, "Leopard!" The monkeys then head for the trees. Another call means, "Eagle!" That makes everyone look up and then dive into thick cover.

Monkeys have many enemies. In Africa, lions and leopards will eat baboons if other prey cannot be found.

33

The bright colors of a male mandrill's face help it attract mates.

34

Massive Mandrills

The biggest monkeys, not just of the Old World but anywhere in the world, are the mandrills. They are found in the tropical rain forests of West Africa.

An adult male mandrill is a fearsome-looking animal, especially when he is on the defensive. He is much larger than a female mandrill, and may stand nearly 3 feet (0.9 m) tall and weigh more than 80 pounds (36 kg). His enormous **canine teeth** are as long and dangerous as those of a lion. The male also has a strikingly colored face. His nose, which is long and red, has bright blue ridges on either side. Beneath his chin, the mandrill has a short yellow beard. The rear view of a male mandrill is nearly as colorful as his face. The monkey has a bare, bluish-purple backside. Female and young mandrills have similar color patterns, but they are not as bright as the males.

Dog-faced Monkeys

Baboons are nearly as big and impressive as mandrills. A male baboon is about the same height as a mandrill—3 feet (1 m) tall—and can weigh more than 55 pounds (25 kg). There are five different baboon species. They are found in the open grasslands of Africa, where they spend most of their life on the ground. Baboons have strong limbs and can easily walk long distances. They usually stay together in large troops.

Baboons have a long, narrow muzzle, similar to that of a dog's. But the teeth of an adult male baboon are much bigger and more scary than any dog's teeth. An angry baboon is dangerous.

The best-known baboon is the hamadryas baboon of northern Africa. Thousands of years ago, in ancient Egypt, the hamadryas baboon was regarded as sacred. Pictures of baboons have been found painted on the walls of tombs. The Egyptians even mummified baboons in the same way that they mummified pharaohs and other important people.

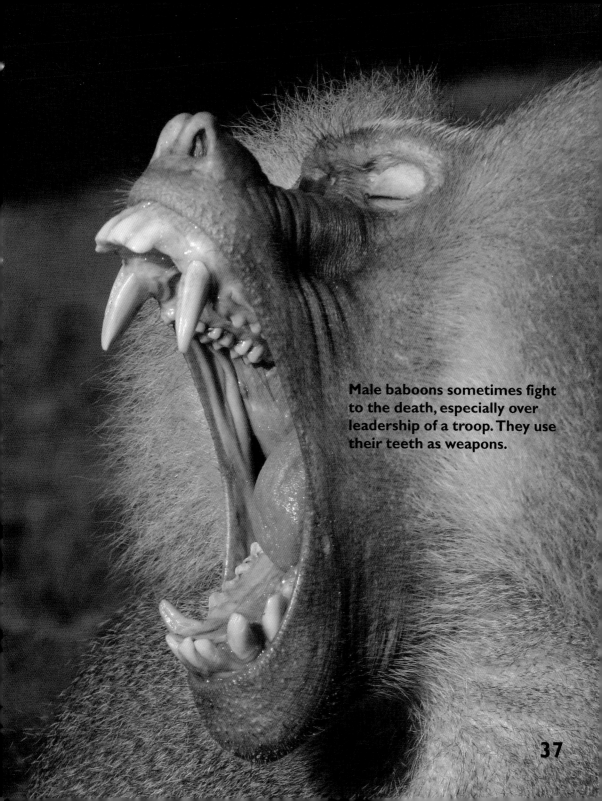

Male baboons sometimes fight to the death, especially over leadership of a troop. They use their teeth as weapons.

The Japanese macaque
lives farther north than any
other nonhuman primate.

Macaques

Throughout many parts of Asia live monkeys called macaques. There are 21 species of macaques and they are all large, sturdily built monkeys. Often, they have names describing the features that help to distinguish one species from another. There are long-tailed macaques, pig-tailed macaques, lion-tailed macaques, bonnet macaques—so-called because of the whorl of hair on their head—and so on. One macaque, called the rhesus monkey, has been much studied by medical scientists. It has given its name to an important factor found in blood.

Most macaques are equally at home living in trees or on the ground. Some species live only in tropical rain forests, while others have adapted to live in colder climates. The Japanese macaque of northern Japan has an extra-thick coat that enables it to survive cold winters. In the areas where those monkeys live, there are natural springs of steaming hot water. The macaques swim and sit in the water to help keep themselves warm.

Long Noses

The riverside and swamp forests of the island of Borneo are home to a large and most unusual monkey. That is the proboscis (PROH-BOSS-ISS) monkey. The word *proboscis* is Greek for "long snout"—and the male monkey certainly lives up to his name. He has a huge, floppy, spoon-shaped nose, which droops down over his mouth and chin. Female and young proboscis monkeys have a much smaller, snub nose.

A big nose is very important to a male proboscis monkey. The larger his nose, the more it attracts the attention of the females. One male might gather as many as seven or eight females, with whom he mates. Proboscis monkeys live together in the trees as a family group.

Proboscis monkeys like to stay near the water and are very good swimmers. They have even been seen swimming underwater.

Male proboscis monkeys
will roar to scare away
other males that come too
close to their family group.

A Hanuman langur's tail can grow to 3½ feet (1.1 m) long.

Sacred Langurs

Some of the most frequently seen monkeys in India and its neighboring countries, such as Pakistan and Sri Lanka, are the langurs. There are three different species and by far the best known are the Hanuman, or gray, langurs.

Hanuman is the name of the Hindu monkey-god. The langurs that are named for him are regarded as sacred in many parts of India. Because people are not allowed to hunt or trap Hanuman langurs, the monkeys often live near to people without fear. They are found not only in the forests, but in towns and villages. Often, the langurs make a nuisance of themselves by stealing food from farms and even from shops.

When Hanuman langurs are not taking human food, they eat mainly leaves. But their natural diet also includes more unusual things, such as the gum from certain trees and a type of fruit containing the poison strychnine (STRICK-NEEN). This fruit is deadly to most animals.

Fine Fur

The colobus monkeys of African forests and woodlands have the most striking coats of all the Old World monkeys. The black colobus monkeys have shiny black fur. Most of them have a contrasting white face. Some also have a "cape" of long, fine white hair that spreads over their shoulders, and a long tail ending in a white tuft. Black colobus babies are usually born snow-white and develop the adult color as they grow. Other species include the red colobus monkeys and the olive colobus monkeys. Colobus monkeys lack thumbs, or have only a tiny stub, but they can still hang onto branches easily as they leap through the trees.

In the 19th century, the fur of the black colobus monkey was in great demand by the fashion trade in Europe. Many monkeys were killed for their coat. Fortunately, today, such slaughter is illegal—although **poachers** still hunt the colobus.

The guereza, or white-mantled black colobus, lives in the rain forests of Africa. Wild chimpanzees often hunt this monkey.

45

Patas monkeys live to about 20 years in the wild. Bigger Old World monkeys, such as mandrills, might live into their 40s.

46

Fast on Their Feet

In the animal world, monkeys are among the best athletes. The fastest monkey is the patas monkey, a ground-dwelling species of the African **savanna**. Slender and graceful, patas monkeys have long legs that carry them at speeds of 35 miles (55 km) an hour. That is faster than many horses can gallop! They have long feet and strong fingers and toes that help them run. The patas monkey is a small animal. Even the males, which are larger than the females, do not usually weigh much more than 20 pounds (9 kg). These small monkeys measure no more than about 30 inches (75 cm) in body length.

Patas monkeys have a shaggy, orange-brown coat with pale underparts. Their face is black and decorated with a white mustache. Their coloring once earned them another name—the hussar monkey. In the 19th century, European visitors to Africa thought that the patas looked like hussars, or military horsemen, in uniform.

Monkeys at Risk

Monkeys are commonly seen in the forests of Africa and Asia, and at first glance appear to be thriving. But the monkeys' future is not as secure as it looks. Everywhere, people are cutting down forests for timber or to clear land for farming. When the trees go, many monkeys lose the **habitat** that they need to survive, and their numbers start to fall. Some species are already rare. If forest clearance continues, many of these monkeys are in great danger of becoming **extinct**.

In many regions, monkeys have other reasons to fear humans. The meat of wild animals, or "bush meat," is popular among some peoples. Monkeys are commonly hunted for food. Also, poachers frequently shoot monkeys for their fur, or trap them to be sold in the pet trade.

Conservationists are working to protect monkeys by setting up **reserves**. That will ensure that certain forests will remain untouched. Such reserves might also help make it easier to control poaching.

Words to Know

Adaptations   Characteristics of animals that make them better suited to their surroundings or diet.

Canine teeth   Long, sharp pointed teeth between the front teeth and the molars.

Conservationists   People who work to keep wildlife and its natural surroundings safe.

Extinct   When all of a type of animal are dead and gone forever.

Fossils   The preserved remains of ancient animals or plants.

Gestation period   The length of time it takes for a young animal to develop inside its mother.

Grooming   Cleaning and tidying the body, including combing fur.

Habitat   The area where an animal or a plant lives naturally.

Mate   To come together to produce young; either of a breeding pair.

Nursing   Feeding on a mother's milk.

Opposable thumb	A thumb that can move across the hand to meet the pads, or tips, of the fingers.
Poachers	People who hunt illegally.
Predators	Animals that hunt other animals.
Prehensile	Describing a tail that can be used for grasping objects.
Prey	An animal hunted by another animal for food.
Primates	A group of mammals that includes lemurs, tarsiers, monkeys, and apes.
Reserves	Areas of land set aside for the protection of animals and plants.
Sacs	Baglike parts of the stomach that are found in some monkeys.
Savanna	Dry grasslands with few trees in Africa.
Species	The scientific word for animals of the same type that breed together.
Territory	The area that an animal regards as its own home.
Troop	A group of monkeys.

Find Out More

Books

Lockwood, S. *Baboons*. The World of Mammals.
Mankato, Minnesota: The Child's World, 2005.

Martin, P. A. F. *Monkeys of Asia and Africa*. True Books.
Danbury, Connecticut: Children's Press, 2000.

Web sites

Baboon
animals.nationalgeographic.com/animals/mammals/
baboon.html
Profile of the olive baboon.

Mandrill
www.enchantedlearning.com/subjects/mammals/monkey/
Mandrillprintout.shtml
Information about mandrills and a picture to print.

Index